We would like to hear from you. Please send your comments to the addresses below. Thank you.

ccpropes@isaiah4310.com
laurabostrom@isaiah4310.com

I AM book
Copyright ©2006, 2007 by
Chrysti Carol Propes and Laura Bostrom.
All rights reserved.

Cover design
Copyright ©2003, 2006, 2007 by
Laura Bostrom. All rights reserved.

Illustrations
Copyright ©2006, 2007
by Laura Bostrom. All rights reserved.

ISBN 978-0-9790791-0-8

Printed at Manipal Press Ltd, India.

"So that you'll come to know and trust me, understand both

that I am

and

who I am."

Isaiah 43:10 (Msg)

Jesus,

We ask you to bless this book and every hand that

touches it. Open the eyes, ears, and hearts of your children so

they can *really* see, hear and *know* you. Thank you for showing us

<u>That You Are & Who You Are.</u>

You are our life!

Laura and Chrysti Carol

For Travis,
I love you.

For Andrew and Ryan,
Look to God in all you do-
and know that no matter what-
God created you for a very special
reason. You are the greatest gifts God
could ever give me.
Love you, Mom

To Marcus R.
I'm blessed by your love,
commitment and belief.
I love you deeply and eternally.

For my beautiful Seth and Helena,
"How I love you…How I love you…You mea
the world to me."Your hearts will beat with
mine- always and forever. Teach your
children and grandchildren *and* their childre
the saving love of Jesus Christ.
I love you! Mom

Believe

See

Know

Trust

I AM

Written by:
Chrysti Carol Propes

Themed and Illustrated by:
Laura Bostrom

I love to be a little child.

To run and play,
to laugh and smile.

I love to climb tall, tall trees.

To play outside,
there's so much to see!

I notice beauty everywhere,
and I have a secret
I'd like to share.

I AM Hope.

Everything your eyes can see
was made by God
for you and me.

I AM Creator.

He made the sun, the moon
and the great big sky.

I AM Forever.

He made the grass, the flowers and the butterflies.

I AM Kind.

He made all the
animals on dry land.

I AM Truth.

He made the ocean,
the fish and
the sand.

I AM Life.

But that's not all
that was in God's plan!

You Are- because | AM

You were made by God's
hands too.

I AM your Father.

The world wouldn't be complete without you.

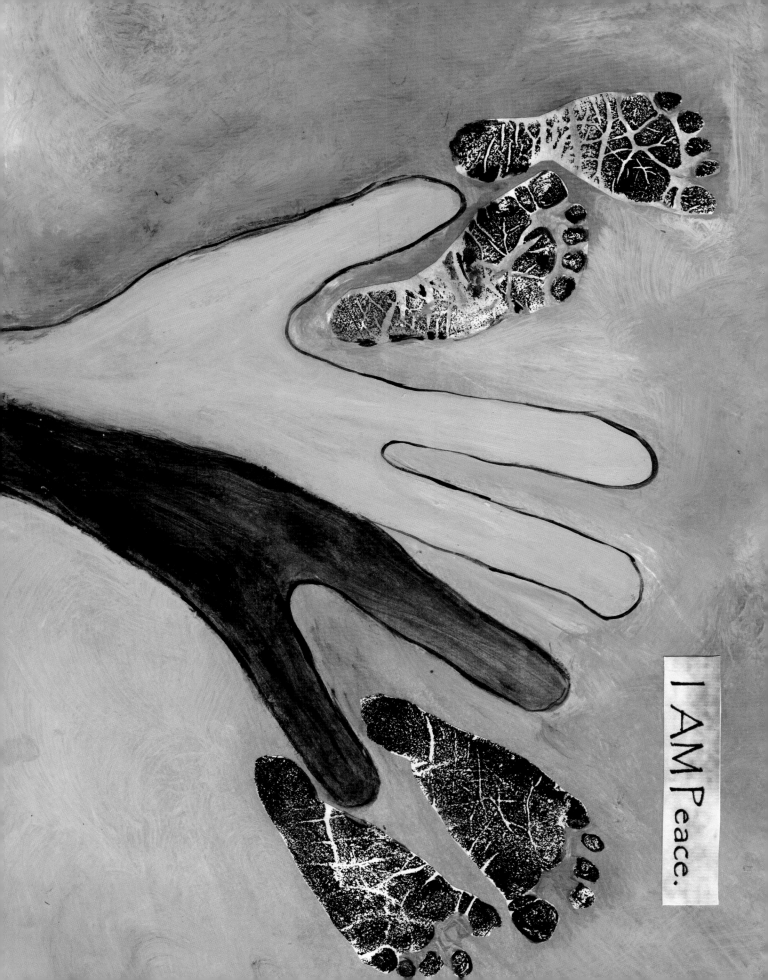

I AM Peace.

So, the next time you play or just sit for awhile, think about this...

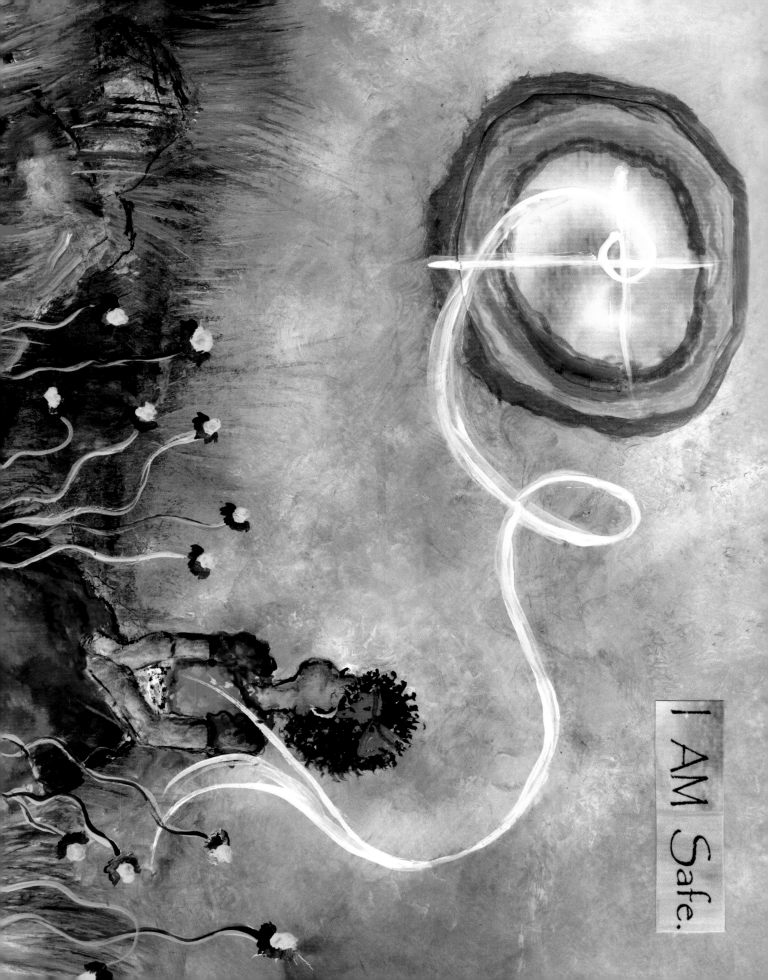

You are God's chosen child!

I AM Good.

"The LORD is good to all;
he has compassion on all he has made.
Psalm 145:9(NIV)

I AM Hope.

"O Lord, you alone are my hope.
I've trusted you, O Lord, from childhood.
Psalm 71:5(NLT)

I AM Creator.

"For you created my inmost being; you knit
me together in my mother's womb. I praise
you because I am fearfully and wonderfully
made; your works are wonderful, I know
that full well." Psalm 139:13-14(NIV)

I AM Real.

"Now faith is being sure of what we hope
for and certain of what we do not see."
Hebrews 11:1(NIV)

I AM Here.

"Wherever you go, I will watch over you,
then later I will bring you back to this land.
I won't leave you--I will do all I have
promised." Genesis 28:15(CEV)

I AM Alive.

"Praise God, the Father of our Lord Jesus
Christ. God is so good, and by raising Jesus
from death, he has given us new life and a
hope that lives on." 1 Peter 1:3(CEV)

I AM Forever.

"Trust in the Lord always,
for the Lord God is the eternal Rock."
Isaiah 26:4(NLT)

I AM Kind.

"But the fruit of the Spirit is love, joy,
peace, patience, kindness, goodness,
faithfulness, gentleness and self control.
Against such things there is no law."
Galatians 5:22-23(NIV)

I AM Truth.

"Pilate said, "So you are a king?"
Jesus responded, "You say I am a king.
Actually, I was born and came into the
world to testify to the truth. All who
love the truth recognize that what I say
is true." John 18:37(NLT)

I AM Life.

"For God so loved the world that he gave his one
and only Son, that whoever believes in him shall
not perish but have eternal life." John 3:16(NIV)

I AM your Father.

"For there is one body and one Spirit, just as
you have been called to one glorious hope for
the future. There is one Lord, one faith, one
baptism, and one God and Father, who is over
all and in all and living through all."
Ephesians 4:4-6(NLT)

I AM Peace.

"I give you peace, the kind of peace that
only I can give. It isn't like the peace that
this world can give. So don't be worried or
afraid." John 14:27(CEV)

I AM Safe.

"I will lie down and sleep in peace,
for you alone, O LORD, make me dwell
in safety." Psalm 4:8(NIV)

We hope you enjoyed this book.
Please share it with everyone you
know and give God all the praise and glory!
This is all for Him and because of Him.

Other I AM books

I AM Here
ISBN 978-0-9790791-1-5

I AM Hope
Available Summer 2007!
ISBN 978-0-9790791-2-2